PHOTOGRAPHY BY KENNETH BERG | TEXT BY BRENDA DUFF

I am Ruth

A Story of Loss, Love & Redemption

First printing: June 2013

ISBN: 978-0-89221-719-9
Library of Congress Number: 2013933184

Photography by Kenneth Berg
Cover and Interior Design by Diana Bogardus

Please consider requesting that a copy of this volume be purchased by your local library system.

Printed in China

Please visit our website for other great titles:
www.newleafpress.net

For information regarding author interviews,
please contact the publicity department at (870) 438-5288

New Leaf Press
A Division of New Leaf Publishing Group
www.newleafpress.net

SPECIAL THANKS

to Zola Levitt Ministries, Elia Sides, Frank Gampel, Bill Elliott, Elinor Flaxman, Eyal Rozales, Yuva Ben Shimol, Itamar Segev, Hani Peretz, The Hashmonean Village, Zohar Bar Am, Mili Rendler, Andrea Davis, and Janell Wimberly.

a photographic journey through the book of Ruth

The scenes portrayed in this book were photographed in the Holy Land, within close proximity to the actual sites where they originally took place nearly three thousand years ago.

Faith

Loyalty

Grace

Restored

FOREWORD

How is it possible that a story written 3,000 years ago could still touch our hearts so deeply and change our lives profoundly when it is retold?

I Am Ruth is a powerful story of loss, love, and redemption that transcends time and space.

I Am Ruth beautifully portrays a basic human truth about suffering and faith. It begins with the friendship of two women grieving the loss of husbands, children, home, and hope.

> "Look," said Naomi to Ruth, "your sister-in-law is going back to her people and her gods. Go back with her."
>
> But Ruth replied, "Don't urge me to leave you or to turn back from you. Where you go I will go, and where you stay I will stay. Your people will be my people and your God my God. Where you die I will die, and there I will be buried. May the Lord deal with me, be it ever so severely, if anything but death separates you and me".
> —Ruth 1:15–17 (NIV)

The love story between Ruth and Boaz, her kinsman redeemer, is a picture of God's love for each of us poured out through the life, death, and resurrection of our Redeemer, Jesus. But this is not the book of Boaz. Ruth is the great-grandmother of David. Both Ruth and Boaz are mentioned in the Messianic genealogy of Matthew 1:5.

But into the tapestry of the redemption story there is a golden thread of hope and loyalty woven throughout the narrative. Shining brightly through the picture of sorrow is the faithful love of two friends, Ruth and Naomi. . . . Their friendship was a bond of love that would not be turned away in the face of hardship.

What a woman Ruth must have been! The kind of friend we all long to have; the kind of strong, loyal person we all long to be! I am reminded that Ruth's great-grandson David inherited Ruth's strength and loyalty. David's friendship and loyalty with Jonathan mirrors that of Ruth for Naomi. Fierce, undying loyalty and love for his friend was a quality that made David "a man after God's own heart."

A thousand years after Ruth traveled to Bethlehem with Naomi, our Lord Jesus was born in the village where love and loyalty and redemption was first defined. Jesus is the only Son of God, but in His humanity He is the son of Mary, descended from Ruth and the long-awaited son of David. He is our kinsman-redeemer. The Lord is also our faithful friend who says to us, like Ruth said to Naomi, "I will never leave you or forsake you!" (Heb. 13:5).

The story of Ruth is ultimately the portrait of God's unfailing love for us no matter how difficult life may be. The story of Ruth proves that the Lord will stick by us through every hardship. Ruth's faithful friendship is a picture of the heart of Jesus. Love that will never be turned back is a quality we see passed down from generation to generation. *I Am Ruth* is the vision of the kind of person we all long to become and the faithful life we long to live.

— Bodie Thoene
Bestselling Author of Christian Fiction
and recipient of ECPA Gold Medallion Awards

Nearing the end of the harvest; the grain heads have been removed, leaving just straw.

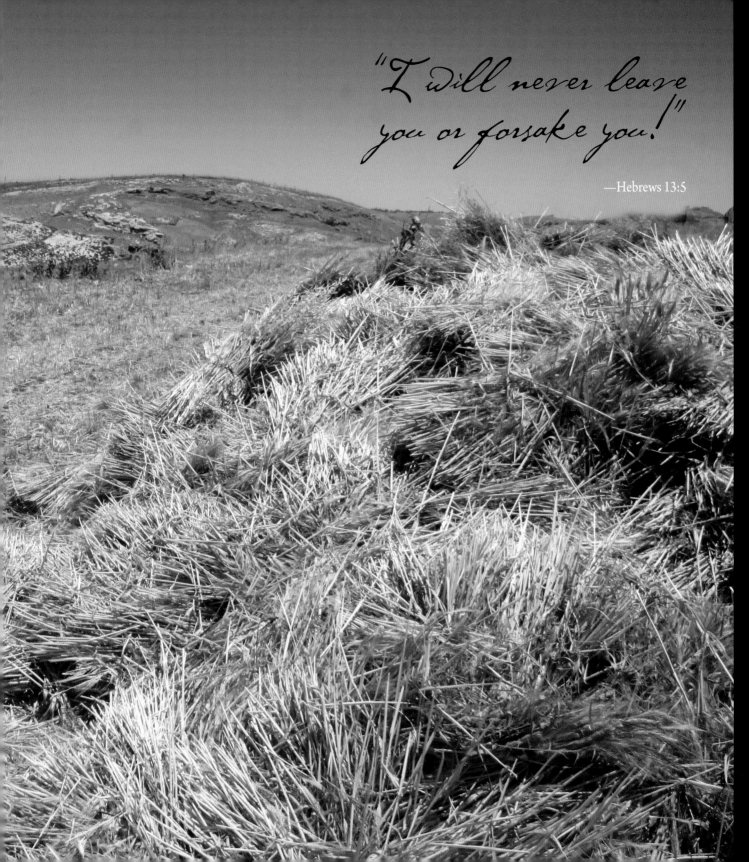

"I will never leave you or forsake you!"

—Hebrews 13:5

OVERVIEW

The biblical Book of Ruth takes place in the middle of the Old Testament journal of Israel. Before Ruth's story, the history of Israel began with God's promise to Abraham of salvation for all nations that would come through the seed of him and his wife Sarah. Then came Abraham's walk by faith through the Promised Land. From there, the geographical history of the Promised Land contributes to the setting and events of God's story told in the Book of Ruth.

With all the kings, pharaohs, tribal leaders, and would-be conquerors of the world, the only true leader was and is God. His plan and timing would remain consistent even in the rejection by His own people to worship glorified stone and metal carved by human hands. With mercy He rescued His people time and time again. During the days of Ruth, God provided guidance through Israel's judges. But the judges themselves would not be enough for His ultimate plan of rescue.

The hills of Judea near Jericho and Qumram, home of the Dead Sea Scrolls. These hills are steep, very dry, and hot, especially in the summer. The area has few residents beyond Bedouins who live very much as they did during biblical times.

FROM LOSS TO HOPE

Through the lives of three people — Naomi, Ruth, and Boaz — God performed an act of redemption that breathes His own personal message of love. His promise to Abraham would be a hallmark in their little town of Bethlehem and God would proceed with His plan from there all the way through Israel's future history to the birth of the Messiah, our Savior.

The dearness of Ruth's story comes through the loss of land and loved ones . . . an abandonment of life and hope. Naomi had known the wonders of God for His people but soon came to know the emptiness of His silence, causing her to search her own heart.

While in the foreign land of Moab, God brought a special young woman into Naomi's life. This young Moabitess named Ruth, together with Naomi, receives a new hope of life through the kinsman redeemer Boaz, all by God's faithful design.

Naomi *Ruth* *Boaz*

A GREATER PLAN AND PURPOSE The love
of God worked its way intricately through all three of their lives bonding them together in His
perfect plan. They would never have reached this sweet union without Him, and could not
know their story was but a stepping stone in a lineage that would lead to Jesus Christ.

Redemption had been a part of His plan all along and through His only begotten Son, Jesus,
the Messiah, came the ultimate redemption of mankind.

*The story of
Ruth is God's story
of loss, love, and
redemption*

On the way to Moab just beyond Bethlehem. Donkeys are still used by those who live in the desert for transportation and work, such as shepherding sheep.

Bethlehem, a small town of the tribe of Judah, was once rich and fertile. The tribe of Judah itself was one of the largest of 12 tribes that settled in the land of Canaan, each representing one of the 12 sons of Jacob who was renamed by God Himself as "Israel." Both names are used throughout the Bible.

Bethlehem began as a tiny town, remained a tiny town throughout history, and is still a tiny town today. This is where the story of Ruth begins, a place where God Himself chose to bring people together in a prelude of His love story that continued through to the birth of Christ and beyond.

The story begins at the onset of a famine. The ancestors of the people known as the children of Israel had experienced famines in the past. In those days there were great leaders who followed God in His plan for rescue — leaders like Joseph, Moses, and Joshua. The leaders at the time of the Book of Ruth were judges who were appointed one by one to rescue the people in the war and conflict that developed with surrounding nations. Some judges are still well-known like Deborah, Gideon, and Samson.

A TIME OF HUNGER Much of the
trouble came when some of the children of Israel mixed their faith in God with the worship of idols from those surrounding pagan nations. Over time, regardless of the judges' successful rescues, the people of Israel turned away time and time again from God and began to decide for themselves what was right. And so their land, dependent on God's rain to be rich and fertile, slowly dried up. Springtime would not bring a crop of barley to harvest. Instead there would be famine, fear, and desperation.

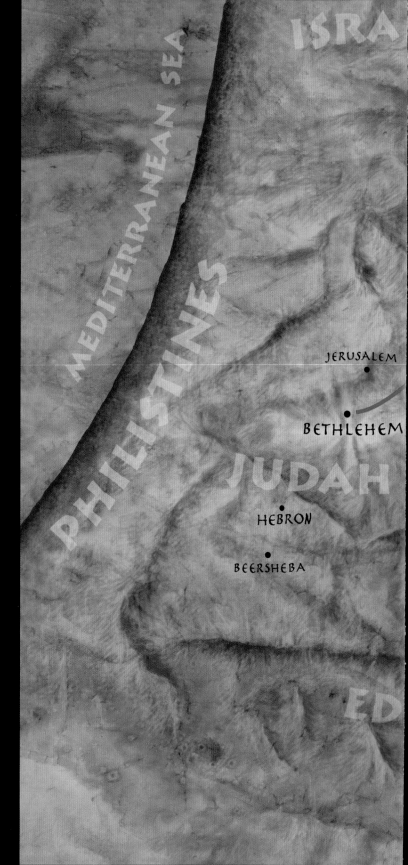

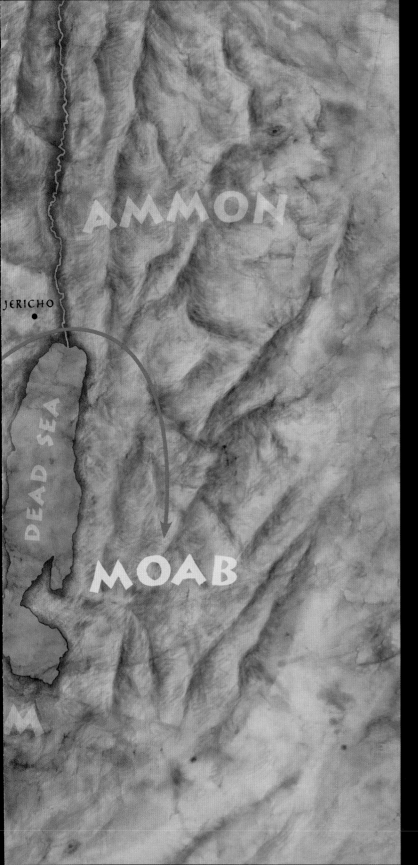

AMMON

JERICHO

DEAD SEA

MOAB

With farming and raising sheep as the main activities that Bethlehem's population relied upon for food and prosperity, the sobering famine endangered everything, leaving no potential for a harvest or the joy of celebration in their hearts. It was such a sad time; they needed direction and mercy. Always in the past God had been so willing to give it, and how He must have grieved for them.

Birds could fly to better places for food, sheep had a shepherd to follow and care for them, but the people would be left to deal with their hunger, not just for food but for the loving care of their living God.

> Now it came to pass, in the days when the judges ruled, that there was a famine in the land. And a certain man of Bethlehem, Judah, went to dwell in the country of Moab, he and his wife and his two sons. The name of the man was Elimelech, the name of his wife was Naomi, and the names of his two sons were Mahlon and Chilion — Ephrathites of Bethlehem, Judah. And they went to the country of Moab and remained there.
>
> –Ruth 1:1–2

A TIME FOR DECISIONS Among

the residents of Bethlehem was a man named Elimelech. He and his wife, Naomi, and their two sons were known as "Ephrathites." The word comes from "Ephrath," meaning "fruitful," which was the ancient name of the land of Bethlehem, which itself means "house of bread." Despite names of the past and present, this would soon no longer be considered a place of abundance.

Elimelech depended on the barley harvest to care for his family, but soon the lands were empty of any stored barley and wheat to make bread. Bethlehem is a city on a hill, with two deep valleys, one to the north and one to the south. From its height, Elimelech could see the mountains of Moab to the east. The spring rains fell more often there, sometimes even snow, and the winds would be cooler.

He faced a difficult decision. Should he take his family there? He looked into the face of his dear, faithful wife, Naomi. He knew that she and their sons would stay with him in Bethlehem or they would leave with him . . . whatever he chose to do.

REMEMBRANCES OF JOSEPH
The famines of God's judgment in the past had lasted for many years. Elimelech looked toward the south. There he could see Hebron about 20 miles away. Jacob was buried there in the field of Machpelah in a cave. It is a double cave that Jacob's grandfather, Abraham, had bought from the Hittites as a place to bury his beloved wife Sarah.

Elimelech remembered from family history that Jacob had left Hebron at one time because of a famine in the land. Jacob had to travel a very long way south and then west to Egypt where waiting anxiously for him was his son Joseph, whom he thought had been killed by a wild animal when he was just a boy. Joseph's brothers had secretly sold him as a slave and then told their father the false story of his death. But God had used the jealousy of his brothers to make Joseph a powerful leader in Egypt, second only to Pharaoh.

God had told Jacob not to be afraid to go to Egypt because He would go with him. Jacob was not worried because God also told him that he would be with his family and would one day bring them all back to the land of Canaan. Pharaoh provided carts for Jacob so he could bring all of his family, their livestock, and possessions to Egypt. Jacob and Joseph's 11 brothers would have food and a place to live in Goshen during the famine.

Rescue had come for Jacob and his sons, but not without much grief and sorrow. Would God be merciful to the children of Israel once again in this famine?

When Jacob died, Pharaoh allowed Joseph to bury his father in Abraham's burial cave where Jacob's mother and father, Rebekah and Isaac, were also buried. There was a great procession to take Jacob's body back to Hebron, with Joseph and his brothers and their entire households except for their little children and flocks left safely behind in Goshen. Joseph was even accompanied by all of Pharaoh's officials, all the senior members of Pharaoh's household, and all the senior officers of Egypt with their great number of chariots and horses.

When they arrived in Canaan, they stopped at the threshing floor of Atad, near the Jordan River, and there they held a great memorial service. For seven days they mourned for Jacob. The Canaanite people, who had been watching nearby, renamed that place "Abel-mizraim" because they thought that it was a place of deep mourning for the Egyptians.

Elimelech, whose name means "My God is King," would have memorized the final words of his ancestor Jacob to his 12 sons, for this historical account had been told from generation to generation. To his son Judah, the father of Elimelech's tribe, Jacob had said:

Judah, you are he whom your brothers shall praise;

Your hand shall be on the neck of your enemies;

Your father's children shall bow down before you.

Judah is a lion's whelp;

From the prey, my son, you have gone up.

He bows down, he lies down as a lion;

And as a lion, who shall rouse him?

The scepter shall not depart from Judah,

Nor a lawgiver from between his feet,

Until Shiloh comes;

And to Him shall be the obedience of the people.

Binding his donkey to the vine,

And his donkey's colt to the choice vine,

He washed his garments in wine,

And his clothes in the blood of grapes.

His eyes are darker than wine,

And his teeth whiter than milk .

—Genesis 49:8–12

Along a narrow path in the rocky hills of Judea. The trees and plants grow because of a nearby water source, possibly a stream or a well. The elevation of the area makes this part of the hills cooler than the lower valleys.

Trusting in God and His word, Elimelech made his decision — they would make the journey to Moab where he and his family could make a living during this time of the famine.

Travel started from the city gate of Bethlehem onto a path that would lead them to the main road, a well-worn path sometimes called the "way." This path would not go through the main cities, but through the desert, wilderness, and rocky slopes. Travelers might be able to keep up with a caravan if arranged and perhaps meet some merchants selling wares along the way. One day's journey, which could be up to 20 miles on foot, was not only tiring but dangerous at times because of thieves hidden from sight.

BEYOND THE SALT SEA

The country of Moab is a land on a plateau that rises gradually from north to south. The gorge or "valley" of the Arnon River is its northern boundary. The white cliffs of the Salt Sea are Moab's western boundary; to the east and the south it is bordered by a circle of hills.

The Salt Sea, which is today called "The Dead Sea," separated Moab from the land of Israel. Elimelech and his family would not be able to cross over to the land of Moab by taking a sailboat because these waters are so thick with salt not even the fish can survive there.

They would have to travel about 60 miles on a four day to one week journey north along the western side of the Salt Sea, cross over the shallow part of the River Jordan eastward, and then journey south to Moab along the east side of the Salt Sea.

The Salt Sea had once been an area much like an oasis, with an abundance of water flowing from the Jordan River. Some of the cities of the plain in the southern part of the Salt Sea had abruptly been destroyed, and the children of Israel and the children of Moab remembered well how it happened.

THE TIME OF ABRAHAM

The events involved the patriarch of the Moabite people named Lot, the nephew of Abraham. All of the children of Abraham and his descendants are cousins of the Moabite children of Lot and his descendants.

Terah was the father of Abraham and all of his family was living in Haran, located north of the Euphrates River in what is today a small Turkish village. They had moved to Haran from their native land in Ur, located in present-day Iraq.

While in Haran, God told Abraham to leave his people. He was to journey to a place that God Himself would show him because it was His plan to make Abraham into a great nation. This is a wonder of God because Abraham was 75 years old and his wife Sarah had not borne him any children. In God's plan, all the families of earth would be blessed in Abraham, and the people who blessed Abraham, God would bless; the people who cursed Abraham, God would curse.

Abraham and his wife Sarah, with all their wealth and the servants of their household, began traveling south. Lot, the son of Abraham's deceased brother, went with them. They would travel as far as they could and then camp. They traveled and camped many times, going a long distance. When they arrived in the land of Canaan, Abraham camped at the first city they came to, which is Shechem. If you went there today you would be at the center of Israel. It was there that God told Abraham that his descendants would inherit the land, and so he built an altar there and worshipped God.

Abraham's family and household continued the journey south and camped in the hill country between the twin cities of Ai to the east and Bethel to the west. He built another altar there and again faithfully worshipped God. They left and continued their journey south to the Negev desert on the southeast side of the Salt Sea.

A severe famine came to the land, so they went all the way southwest to Egypt for food. Sarah's beauty won the attention of the pharaoh, and a deception about her identity took place, but God prevented anything from happening to Sarah or Abraham because of His plan to give them descendants. God brought a plague on the pharaoh, but in His mercy warned him that it was because Sarah was the wife of Abraham.

Pharaoh made them leave with all their possessions which included the gifts the pharaoh had given Abraham when he took Sarah into his palace. The couple and their family traveled back through the Negev and up to Bethel where Abraham had built an altar, and he worshipped God yet again.

An ancient olive tree, hundreds of years old. There are lots of olive trees in the higher mountain areas, and if cut down, their strong root systems can produce new trees.

A Fateful Choice

Lot's and Abraham's shepherds began to argue over grazing land because their flocks and herds had grown large in number. Abraham did not want them to fight . . . they were family. He told his nephew Lot that it would be best for them to separate. If Lot stayed to the west, Abraham said he would go east. If Lot went to the east, Abraham said he would stay to the west. He gave Lot a choice of lands.

Lot saw how beautiful and well-watered the plains of the Jordan were, so he chose to journey eastward. Abraham stayed in the west and moved his tents to Hebron. Lot lived in the cities of the plains of the Jordan as far south as the city of the Canaanite people called "Sodom." It was a wicked city, and the people did evil toward God. Abraham had to rescue Lot from four mighty kings that had captured him in a battle with the king of Sodom and four other kings.

It was some time after Lot's rescue that God told Abraham and Sarah they would have a son. Sarah gave her handmaid Hagar to Abraham to have a child, thinking this must be how it should happen since she and Abraham were getting much older. Abraham had a child with Hagar and he was named Ishmael. Abraham loved Ishmael very much but God's plan was for Abraham to have a son with Sarah. This is when God Himself changed Abraham's name from "Abram" and Sarah's name from "Sarai." God did this to signify that Abraham and Sarah would be the father and mother of many nations.

At the same time God told them of the promised son, he warned Abraham of the impending doom to come on Sodom. The wickedness of Sodom and the neighboring city of Gomorrah had become so great that God could hear the outcry against them. Abraham had cared for his brother's son Lot as his own and he asked God to spare the city of Sodom. But there were not even ten righteous people living there, just Lot and his wife and two daughters, so the city was not to be spared.

God was going to rain fire and brimstone down on the cities. The bitumen pits, a natural petroleum product similar to asphalt, were in the shallow part of the Salt Sea near the cities. The shower of fire and brimstone would ignite the bitumen and explode the cities with fire.

All of this was about to happen quickly, but God in His mercy sent the two angels who were about to destroy the cities to warn Lot. After the angels had seen the city's wickedness they told Lot the next morning to leave quickly with his family. The angels took Lot and his wife and two daughters by the hand and rushed them out of the city. When they reached the plains the angels told them to run to mountains and take shelter, to run for their lives and not to look behind them.

Lot did not understand the gravity of the destruction and asked the angels if they could go to the small city of Zoar nearby. It was approved but they were inches away from being included in the destruction from God's judgment.

No sooner had they reached the edge of Zoar than the fire and brimstone fell on the bitumen, and the explosions and bursts of fire destroyed all the plains and the people in it, as well as all vegetation that had grown on the ground.

Sadly, Lot's wife did stop to look back and became hardened with salt. The Bible describes her as turning into a "pillar of salt." Lot and his daughters just barely escaped. The smell of burning sulfur would linger for a very long time, reminding all of these cities' destruction.

Elimelech too may have felt like he was fleeing — fleeing for his life and for the lives of his wife and two sons. The family, small in number, entered Moab. There had been conflicts between the people, all distant cousins in the past, but this was a time of peaceful interaction.

There seemed to be a mixture of the worship of idols in Moab with those who worshiped God. But their worship of God was in the name of Moab's main god . . . Chemosh. They thought God spoke to them through this carved image in stone that they had created. At times they even sacrificed their children in order to get a response from the lifeless idol, even though God said that He never asked for this to be done.

As well as a mix of religious practices, even the language of the people of Moab was mixed with their native Hebrew. The tribe of Reuben from the children of Israel lived near Moab, but were located on the north side of the Arnon River. It may be that Elimelech's family would see some of them in town. The town of Moab was also a place where merchants stopped who had been traveling on the famous "King's Highway," a long highway that goes from Egypt to Damascus, winding through the hills farther to the east of Moab. For now, the family was safe, but they too were far away from their homeland in Bethlehem.

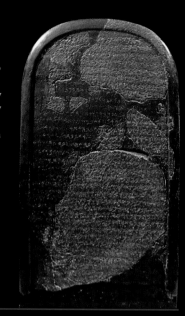

The Mesha Stele, also called the "Moabite Stone," discovered by a German missionary named F.A. Klein in 1868 at Dibon, which is about 20 miles east of the Dead Sea. The stone is inscribed by Mesha, king of Moab of the late ninth century B.C. in which he proclaims victory in the name of their Moabite god "Chemosh."

Then, tragically, Elimelech died. Naomi not only lost connection with her land, she lost the one she had depended on, her husband. Tragedy would soon overwhelm the grieving woman.

Her sons, Mahlon and Chilion, were not well. Mahlon means "weak" and Chilion means "sickly." Since names were sometimes changed, especially when telling their story, the brothers may have suddenly become sick or they may have been weak and sickly at birth. They would marry women of Moab. Chilion chose a woman named Orpah and Mahlon chose a woman named Ruth, but neither woman bore any children in ten years.

First Naomi lost her land, then she lost her husband, and now hope was fading for there to be any descendants of Elimelech. But worse would soon befall the small family. Her only children, Mahlon and Chilion, also died. In her shock and profound anguish, Naomi wondered why God had left her to be the only survivor of her family. Thoughts of God dealing her such hard blows pressed in on her, and her mourning turned into bitterness of heart. Any hope Naomi had left was nearly lost.

Ruth and Orpah still lived with Naomi. There was something about her that made them stay. Their futures were very uncertain; their present was one of loss and grief.

> Then Elimelech, Naomi's husband, died; and she was left, and her two sons. Now they took wives of the women of Moab: the name of the one was Orpah, and the name of the other Ruth. And they dwelt there about ten years. Then both Mahlon and Chilion also died; so the woman survived her two sons and her husband.
>
> —Ruth 1:3–5

RETURNING HOME

The promise God gave to Jacob that He would be with his descendants was still in effect. It may have seemed that God wasn't there. However, His promises are sure, and He certainly was with the children of Israel in their tragedies even though He had not spoken to them in a long while.

Word finally came, all the way from Bethlehem to Moab, and all the way to Naomi. God had visited the people in Bethlehem with a harvest, with bread. This meant that there would be prosperity again!

Naomi rose with her daughters-in-law and they walked out of the city onto the way to Bethlehem. There was no more famine in Bethlehem, but there was still a devastating famine in Naomi's heart and her faith. Yet, like a magnet, God was pulling her, pulling her through her confusion and pain, and most of all pulling her through the feeling of hopelessness.

On the "way" they neared the shallow part of the Jordan River, the place of crossing over from Moab to the promised land of Abraham. It was there long ago that a 40-year journey of the 12 tribes of Israel had ended from their wandering in the desert. These were the descendants of Jacob that God had promised He would bring out of Egypt back to the land He had given Abraham. That is why it is called "The Promised Land."

Near Mt. Nebo, an area that Elimelech's family would have had to pass on the way to Moab. Terraces along the hills are common in the area today, and are used to grow fruits and vegetables. Many date back to the time of Abraham.

When the 12 tribes of the 12 sons of Jacob, known as Hebrews, came to Egypt because of the famine, they were in good relations with the pharaoh. But that changed when years had passed and a new pharaoh became fearful that the large number of the tribes would join his enemies. He made them slaves and gave an order to throw all the male babies in the Nile River.

But there was one newborn from the tribe of Levi that was put in a basket by his mother and placed in the Nile; a baby that the pharaoh's daughter, a princess, found and called Moses, because she had "drawn him out of the water." What did it matter if just one Hebrew baby boy lived? God again had a plan that He would bring to fulfillment through this child.

Moses' own mother was hired to nurture him and the princess raised him in the splendor and ways of the Egyptians. When he had grown, he went to visit his Hebrew people and saw an Egyptian taskmaster beating one of the Hebrews. In anger, Moses killed the Egyptian and fled east to the deserts of Midian. He married Zipporah, the daughter of the priest of Midian, and they had two sons.

There were not many men Moses' age, if any at all, because of the wicked pharaoh's murderous plan to stop the tribes from growing. The pharaoh died and God's plan was still in effect. He sent Moses back to Egypt to rescue the children of Israel out of the enslaving hand of the new pharaoh. God knew what it would take to make this pharaoh release them and He used Moses to bring ten different plagues on Egypt. Many miracles happened in this time in history and the descendants of the children of Israel through every generation have told their children what happened, and the descendants still tell their children today, once a year, at Passover.

Moses led the children of Israel all the way to the edge of the very land that was promised to Abraham and it was necessary that they cross over the Jordan in the Valley of Moab to get there. It was there that Moses, now 120 years old, spoke to the people of Israel, for he was not going with them across the Jordan into the land of Canaan. Instead, he gave them God's instructions, encouraged and blessed them, appointing Joshua, who had assisted him all along the journey, as their new leader.

Moses went up to Mount Nebo and climbed to the peak of Pisgah and God showed him the wonderful land where Abraham, Isaac, and Jacob walked. And Moses died in the land of Moab. No one knows the exact place, but later he was buried by God Himself in a valley near Beth Peor in Moab. At the Jordan, there at the Valley of Moab, the people of Israel mourned for Moses for 30 days.

Naomi could almost hear the cries of the people echoing in the valley because they would leave their beloved leader behind. She became overwhelmed as they walked. If tears could flood her heart, she would drown in the sorrow of leaving her beloved husband, her only sons, and a once-promising future for her family behind.

Then she arose with her daughters-in-law that she might return from the country of Moab, for she had heard in the country of Moab that the Lord had visited His people by giving them bread. Therefore she went out from the place where she was, and her two daughters-in-law with her; and they went on the way to return to the land of Judah.

—Ruth 1:6–7

A CONNECTION TO JERICHO

Naomi's journey was one upon and near lands that were prominent in the history of her people. Across the Jordan River were the plains of what once was the city of Jericho. It was also the harvest season when the children of Israel's new leader Joshua led them across the river.

Before he did though, he also sent two men across the Jordan to spy out the land and the city of Jericho. In Jericho they came upon a Canaanite family whose house was on the city wall in the fortified city. The man's daughter was named Rahab and she hid the spies overnight under stalks of flax on their roof from the king of Jericho, who came to her looking for them. She told him they had been there, but she had seen them leave just as the city gate was closing. When the king left she went up to roof and talked to the spies. She said,

> I know that the Lord has given you the land, that the terror of you has fallen on us, and that all the inhabitants of the land are fainthearted because of you. For we have heard how the Lord dried up the water of the Red Sea for you when you came out of Egypt, and what you did to the two kings of the Amorites who were on the other side of the Jordan, Sihon and Og, whom you utterly destroyed. And as soon as we heard these things, our hearts melted; neither did there remain any more courage in anyone because of you, for the Lord your God, He is God in heaven above and on earth beneath. Now therefore, I beg you, swear to me by the Lord, since I have shown you kindness, that you also will show kindness to my father's house, and give me a true token, and spare my father, my mother, my brothers, my sisters, and all that they have, and deliver our lives from death.
>
> —Joshua 2:9–13

The spies agreed, and Rahab took a scarlet cord and used it to let them down from her window. She also warned them to hide in the mountain for three days until the king had stopped looking for them.

As the "token" Rahab requested, the spies told her to bind the scarlet cord in her window where it could be seen so that her life and the lives of her family would be saved when they came back to take the

city. Rahab believed that the God of the Israelites was the true God, and had rescued the spies. God saw her faith and rescued her and her family.

Naomi's husband Elimelech was related to the courageous woman Rahab who had made Israel's God her God. Would these daughters-in-law of hers make the God of Israel their God? Would their faith be born in a time of Naomi's bitterness?

Naomi suddenly stopped walking and turned to Orpah and Ruth. Grateful for the kindness they had given to her sons and also to her, she wanted them to find new husbands. She told them to go back and return to their own mother's house. Naomi kissed them and they wept aloud saying that they would go with her to her people in Bethlehem.

A second time, Naomi told them to go back, explaining to them that they would not want to go back with her to Bethlehem without husbands. She tried to help them understand that even if she got a husband that night and miraculously had sons, they would not want to be without a husband until the sons were grown. Naomi could not replace her sons and how it grieved her that in her thinking, the hand of God was against her. And she didn't want Ruth and Orpah to face this same lonely future.

They wept aloud again, but this time Orpah's true feelings for her people and her gods were revealed though she might not have realized it herself until then. Orpah, whose name means "the back of the neck," gave Naomi a kiss of farewell and left. But not Ruth — she physically clung to Naomi

For the third time, Naomi said go back. She told Ruth to look at her sister-in-law going back to her people and to her gods. She told Ruth to go and return with her. At this point Ruth, whose name means "friend," reveals her true feelings. Passionately she replies to Naomi:

"Entreat me not to leave you,

Or to turn back from following after you;

For wherever you go, I will go;

And wherever you lodge, I will lodge;

Your people shall be my people,

And your God, my God.

Where you die, I will die,

And there will I be buried.

The LORD do so to me, and more also,

If anything but death parts you and me"

–Ruth 1:16–17

When Ruth had shown that she really meant it, Naomi said no more. Ruth, the descendant of Lot, had refused to leave Naomi, the descendant of Abraham, and they joined together on the journey back to "the promised land."

After days of travel in rugged terrain, as they got nearer to the road of Bethlehem, the dusty road began to be surrounded with the beauty of a land filled with flowers, and hills and fields full of barley ready for the harvest. These were the fields and hills where Naomi and Elimelech had watched their sons play and grow to be men. They flourished with life despite the barrenness of Naomi's heart.

She would be returning through the city's gate without them. However, Ruth was still a young woman; and now, Naomi knew that Ruth could be married to one of the young Israelite men since she had made it known that she had truly become one of them.

Now the two of them went until they came to Bethlehem. And it happened, when they had come to Bethlehem, that all the city was excited because of them.

The people of the tiny town saw Naomi and could not believe it was her. A group of women near her said "Is this Naomi?" Naomi knew she had changed, and wondered why they would still call her Naomi, which means "pleasant." No, they should call her "Mara," which means "bitter," she told them because she had left Bethlehem full but God had afflicted her and brought her back empty . . . she could not give Elimelech an heir now . . . or so she thought. As had happened so many times before in lives of God's people, there was a hope Naomi had yet to even realize, and it would again be someone from a foreign people that would serve His purpose and be part of His plan being fulfilled.

So Naomi returned, and Ruth the Moabitess her daughter-in-law with her, who returned from the country of Moab. Now they came to Bethlehem at the beginning of barley harvest .

—Ruth 1:22

Ruth

1

Elimelech's Family Goes to Moab

[1] Now it came to pass, in the days when the judges ruled, that there was a famine in the land. And a certain man of Bethlehem, Judah, went to dwell in the country of Moab, he and his wife and his two sons. [2] The name of the man *was* Elimelech, the name of his wife *was* Naomi, and the names of his two sons *were* Mahlon and Chilion—Ephrathites of Bethlehem, Judah. And they went to the country of Moab and remained there. [3] Then Elimelech, Naomi's husband, died; and she was left, and her two sons. [4] Now they took wives of the women of Moab: the name of the one *was* Orpah, and the name of the other Ruth. And they dwelt there about ten years. [5] Then both Mahlon and Chilion also died; so the woman survived her two sons and her husband.

Naomi Returns with Ruth

[6] Then she arose with her daughters-in-law that she might return from the country of Moab, for she had heard in the country of Moab that the LORD had visited His people by giving them bread. [7] Therefore she went out from the place where she was, and her two daughters-in-law with her; and they went on the way to return to the land of Judah. [8] And Naomi said to her two daughters-in-law, "Go, return each to her mother's house. The LORD deal kindly with you, as you have dealt with the dead and with me. [9] The LORD grant that you may find rest, each in the house of her husband."

So she kissed them, and they lifted up their voices and wept. [10] And they said to her, "Surely we will return with you to your people."

[11] But Naomi said, "Turn back, my daughters; why will you go with me? *Are* there still sons in my womb, that they may be your husbands? [12] Turn back, my daughters, go—for I am too old to have a husband. If I should say I have hope, *if* I should have a husband tonight and should also bear sons, [13] would you wait for them till they were grown? Would you restrain yourselves from having husbands? No, my daughters; for it grieves me very much for your sakes that the hand of the LORD has gone out against me!"

[14] Then they lifted up their voices and wept again; and Orpah kissed her mother-in-law, but Ruth clung to her.

[15] And she said, "Look, your sister-in-law has gone back to her people and to her gods; return after your sister-in-law." [16] But Ruth said:
"Entreat me not to leave you,
Or to turn back from following after you;
For wherever you go, I will go;
And wherever you lodge, I will lodge;
Your people *shall* be my people,
And your God, my God.
[17] Where you die, I will die,
And there will I be buried.
The LORD do so to me, and more also,
If *anything but* death parts you and me."

[18] When she saw that she was determined to go with her, she stopped speaking to her.

[19] Now the two of them went until they came to Bethlehem. And it happened, when they had come to Bethlehem, that all the city was excited because of them; and the women said, "*Is* this Naomi?"

[20] But she said to them, "Do not call me Naomi;[a] call me Mara,[b] for the Almighty has dealt very bitterly with me. [21] I went out full, and the LORD has brought me home again empty. Why do you call me Naomi, since the LORD has testified against me, and the Almighty has afflicted me?"

[22] So Naomi returned, and Ruth the Moabitess her daughter-in-law with her, who returned from the country of Moab. Now they came to Bethlehem at the beginning of barley harvest.

a   Ruth 1:20 Literally *Pleasant*
b   Ruth 1:20 Literally *Bitter*

Loyalty

chapter two
Hope Finds a Home

The town of Bethlehem must have looked strange to Naomi. The lives of her beloved husband and sons were only memories to those living in their hometown. There were many familiar faces . . . but they were staring at her as if she were a refugee.

At this point in the Bible's story of Ruth the narrator lets us know that Naomi still has family there. She has a close relative, or "kinsman" as they would say, of her husband's family, who is named Boaz. He is an honorable man of great wealth and is mentioned in the Gospel of Matthew as the son of Rahab,[a] the courageous young woman of Jericho mentioned in the previous chapter. Lineage, or an individual's ancestry, in the Bible is very important. It creates a connection to previous generations, and in the case of Boaz in the Book of Ruth, it becomes a vital link in the family line of Jesus Christ all the way back to Abraham.

While Naomi would view Bethlehem as one returning home in grief, Ruth would look at the town and the people she had claimed as her own much differently. She was in a different land, among a different people, and both her future and that of Naomi had to seem very precarious. Yet, as noted earlier, Ruth was determined and made an important, lifelong commitment to Naomi. She had to sense the aching of Naomi returning to her homeland with nothing, the woman she had come to love, the woman she had left her own mother for, a woman who must have powerfully influenced her in terms of a strong faith in God before Naomi's own grief and loss became bitterness. Ruth stayed close to her and though Naomi no longer had her sons, Ruth would look to the needs of her chosen mother even in this new land.

A New Beginning

The children of Israel were just coming out of a famine, always a time of thanksgiving — but Naomi and Ruth were going to need food if they were to survive. Remembering the fields they had walked through on the way in to Bethlehem, Ruth asked Naomi one morning if she could go and glean heads of grain behind someone who would show her favor. This was an important tradition related to the Book of Deuteronomy, which provided laws for all aspects of Jewish life, including provisions for the poor and widowed to have access to food by their own labor in the fields.[b]

Turning to Ruth, in the absence of her own sons to care for her, Naomi replies, "Go, my daughter." This biblical moment tells us something more about the character of Ruth. She is willing to work hard to provide for Naomi and go into the fields by herself so Naomi would not have to do such labor. She is also hopeful that someone will be kind and allow her to work.

The biblical text tells us that Ruth went immediately to the nearest field of reapers. She asked the servant in charge of the workers if she could glean there. The servant knew Ruth was the Moabite woman who had come into town with Naomi and he let her glean.

Ruth would have began working in one of the corners of the field that morning. There were other poor people and some foreigners working there. The field owners allowed them to pick up what had been left behind by the hired reapers because of God's command through Moses that provided for the poor.[c]

Ruth gathered diligently and only stopped once briefly to rest in the shelter. She was not one to "eat the bread of idleness."[d] Although foreigners were also allowed to glean there, she had sought permission or favor to glean from someone in charge. There were plenty favors because of her beauty, but Ruth made it known that she was here to work by her actions and diligence.

A prominent-looking man riding on a horse came up to the field. He was the owner and had come from Bethlehem to check on his fields and the harvest. Ruth did not realize that she was working in Boaz's field or that he was the kinsman of Naomi.

What an unusual and godly man he was. He got off of his horse and blessed the reapers saying, "The Lord be with you!" They answered him, "The Lord bless you!"[e]

A Man of Wealth and Character

Boaz was a kind, strong, and diligent man, who kept his field well under control. His grandfather Nahshon was the warrior leader of the tribe of Judah's army, appointed by God Himself in the desert a year after the children of Israel made their exodus out of Egypt. There were 12 leaders appointed, each for their forefather's tribe. Judah's tribe, the largest of the tribes, along with the tribe of Issachar and Zebulon led the way under their banners from camp to camp, ready for battle if needed.[f] It is not surprising that Boaz had the qualities of a great leader as well. His field was filled with busy people, chopping barley, heaving bundles, beating out the grain, and on the field's corners were the poor and foreigners gathering what was left behind.

In the mass of workers Boaz turns his attention to Ruth. He wants to know about her and asks his servant in charge of the reapers, "Whose young woman is this?" The servant tells Boaz she is the Moabite woman who had come into town with Naomi. She had asked him early that morning if she could glean and he had watched her work all day only stopping once to rest.

e   Ruth 2:4.
f   Numbers 1:1–16 and 2:1–7.

Boaz approaches Ruth. He wants her to know that she, as a young maiden, could be in a dangerous situation if she were to work in another man's field that had no control over the young men. Ruth is aware that she is not like one of Boaz' maidservants working in the field under his protection . . . yet he speaks to her as if she is one of them, "You will listen, my daughter, will you not? Do not go to glean in another field, nor go from here, but stay close by my young women. Let your eyes be on the field which they reap, and go after them. Have I not commanded the young men not to touch you? And when you are thirsty, go to the vessels and drink from what the young men have drawn."[g]

By his comments, Boaz has gone beyond what was biblically required of him. He allowed Ruth to glean in the field, but he is also offering protection from harm, water when she needs it, and a concern for her wellbeing as he has shown for his own workers.

Ruth realizes she has received kindness from this stranger and is curious why. She could not look into his eyes and speak to him, so she fell to the ground and bowed her head saying, "Why have I found favor in your eyes, that you should take notice of me, since I am a foreigner?"

Boaz told Ruth that it had been reported to him what she had done for Naomi since Mahlon died. He had found out that she had left her father and mother and the land of her birth and come here, to people she had not known before. This is noteworthy to the children of Israel that Ruth did something like this, for their patriarch Abraham also had left his mother and father and the land where he was born, with its idols, to come to a place and people he had never known because he believed in God.

Boaz acknowledges her conversion by saying, "The Lord repay your work, and a full reward be given you by the Lord God Israel, under whose wings you have come for refuge."[h] The phrase "Under whose wings you have come for refuge" is a synonym for a convert to the faith.[i]

Ruth had left home that morning hoping to find the one who would give her favor. Boaz' acknowledgment of her love for Naomi and of her conversion let Ruth know that he was the one in whom she wanted favor. So she said to him, "Let me find favor in your sight, my lord; for you have comforted me, and have spoken kindly to your maidservant, though I am not like one of your maidservants."[j]

In this way Ruth acknowledges the kindness she has been shown. Hundreds of years later, Queen Esther would seek the favor of her husband, the king of Persia, as she was about to tell him she was one of his captives from the land of Israel . . . a Jew. God put Esther there to be used in His plan to rescue the Jewish people from the foreign king's own hand. Likewise, God had a plan for both Ruth and Boaz, as well as Naomi, already set in motion that neither could yet see.

Boaz not only gave Ruth favor as one of his maidservants, he invited her to the meal with the reapers. This may have made some of the reapers and maidservants wonder why Boaz would do such a thing for a stranger who was also a foreigner. But this is Boaz' field; he is in command and it is his decision to offer this generosity.

h   Ruth 2:12
i   Torah.org "A World of Kindness: An Analysis of Megillat Ruth (III)" By Yitzchak Etshalom;
     "Dialogue A: Boaz and Ruth" — referencing MT Bikkurim 4:3.
j   Ruth 2:13.

Despite the rocks, this soil is very rich and the climate good for raising wheat and barley. The rocks that are cleared from the field are often used to build terraces and fences that surround the farmland, which would be owned by various families living in the area. A fascinating blend of old and modern can be seen in planting and cultivating the fields.

"Come here, and eat of the bread, and dip your piece of bread in the vinegar,"[k] he told Ruth. She sat down with the reapers and Boaz passed her some parched grain, a meal of baked or toasted kernels. Parched grain was a good staple for the people of Israel. It was like having cereal.

Ruth must have been very hungry, having worked so hard and long. She ate enough bread and grain to give her more strength, but notice some of what she was given was not eaten and she saved it. Clearly Ruth was thinking of Naomi being at home without food, even as she herself was able to eat. Ruth could have stopped working for the day and gone home, but she did not take advantage of Boaz' favor, going instead back out to the fields.

When Ruth left to work, Boaz gave a command to his young men, "Let her glean even among the sheaves, and do not reproach her. Also let grain from the bundles fall purposely for her; leave it that she may glean, and do not rebuke her."[l] The reapers and maidservants may have been surprised at this, but they knew that what Boaz said should be done would be done. Again, Boaz shows Ruth favor by allowing her to glean in areas and ways not required by the biblical law that would enable her to gather more.

Ruth not only had the grain she gleaned since morning, she now had her pick of the stalks and bundles left for her on purpose, not knowing that Boaz had commanded this. She took all that her arms could hold. The reapers said nothing. Ruth kept working until it started to get dark. She had so much barley that she needed to beat the grains out with a stick so that she could carry it. It turned out to be an ephah of barley. That's about 35 pounds!

She gathered it all up and carried the heavy load all the way from the field to the city, anxious to show Naomi the blessings of God upon her that day! She got home and there was her beloved Naomi waiting for her. Naomi must have been hungry too by this time, and Ruth pulled out the bread and parched grain she had saved from the meal and gave it to her.

k   Ruth 2:14.
l.   Ruth 2:15–16.

ONE WHO TOOK NOTICE

Naomi looked at the abundance of grain Ruth had brought. The bitterness and hopelessness in Naomi's heart surely started to weaken. It had been a long time since she had seen so much grain and it was in the arms of her foreign daughter Ruth. Who would have allowed her to work in his field? Who would have showed her so much favor for her to bring home 35 pounds of barley? This much did not come from gleaning the meager grains fallen from the reapers in the corners of the field.

Naomi asked Ruth where she had gleaned and said, "Blessed be the one who took notice of you."[m] It would not have been unusual for a field owner to allow a Hebrew woman to work in his field, but for an owner to take notice of a foreign girl in such a generous way was loosening Naomi's tight fist of contention toward God as she spoke a blessing upon this person.

"The man's name with whom I worked today is Boaz,"[n] Ruth answered.

This was not just any field owner's favor; this was favor from God Himself. At this point Naomi comes back to life in her relationship with God. The man Boaz was her dead husband's close relative. Who but God would do such a thing for her? Naomi now praises God,

"...Blessed be he of the Lord, who has not forsaken His kindness to the living and the dead!..."

–Ruth 2:20

m   Ruth 2:19.
n   Ibid.

Gleaners followed behind the reapers gathering stalks of grain and would pull out the heads of grain from barley or wheat that had been dropped.

A sudden change was coming over Naomi that Ruth had not seen before. It was wonderful that God had blessed them with food, but what did she mean that the Lord had not forsaken the kindness of the living and the dead? Naomi explained, "This man is a relation of ours, one of our close relatives."°

Boaz was not only a relative, he was a close relative, close enough that he could possibly be the one who would buy back her husband's land by marrying her daughter-in-law Ruth. It was already publicly known that Ruth had converted, which made her a widow eligible for redemption.

Naomi's mind was racing with thoughts. God had provided an inheritance law through Moses for women like her who had no sons:

"If a man dies and has no son, then you shall cause his inheritance to pass to his daughter. If he has no daughter, then you shall give his inheritance to his brothers. If he has no brothers, then you shall give his inheritance to his father's brothers. And if his father has no brothers, then you shall give his inheritance to the relative closest to him in his family, and he shall possess it." And it shall be to the children of Israel

A Renewed Faith
Naomi must have realized that God's presence had been with her all along and so she gained control of herself, pulling out of the long depression. Clearly, God was working out a plan and so she began to work with Him in helping Ruth to do what was necessary to fulfill that plan.

She confirmed Boaz' instructions to Ruth, "It is good, my daughter, that you go out with his young women, and that people do not meet you in any other field."ʳ This was good instruction from Naomi. When the harvesters saw Ruth, they would know that she only worked in Boaz' field and no other; this way she would remain under

Ruth Meets Boaz

[1] There was a relative of Naomi's husband, a man of great wealth, of the family of Elimelech. His name was Boaz. [2] So Ruth the Moabitess said to Naomi, "Please let me go to the field, and glean heads of grain after *him* in whose sight I may find favor."

And she said to her, "Go, my daughter."

[3] Then she left, and went and gleaned in the field after the reapers. And she happened to come to the part of the field *belonging* to Boaz, who *was* of the family of Elimelech.

[4] Now behold, Boaz came from Bethlehem, and said to the reapers, "The LORD *be* with you!"

And they answered him, "The LORD bless you!"

5 Then Boaz said to his servant who was in charge of the reapers, "Whose young woman *is* this?"

6 So the servant who was in charge of the reapers answered and said, "It *is* the young Moabite woman who came back with Naomi from the country of Moab. 7 And she said, 'Please let me glean and gather after the reapers among the sheaves.' So she came and has continued from morning until now, though she rested a little in the house."

8 Then Boaz said to Ruth, "You will listen, my daughter, will you not? Do not go to glean in another field, nor go from here, but stay close by my young women. 9 *Let* your eyes *be* on the field which they reap, and go after them. Have I not commanded the young men not to touch you? And when you are thirsty, go to the vessels and drink from what the young men have drawn."

10 So she fell on her face, bowed down to the ground, and said to him, "Why have I found favor in your eyes, that you should take notice of me, since I *am* a foreigner?"

11 And Boaz answered and said to her, "It has been fully reported to me, all that you have done for your mother-in-law since the death of your husband, and *how* you have left your father and your mother and the land of your birth, and have come to a people whom you did not know before. 12 The LORD repay your work, and a full reward be given you by the LORD God of Israel, under whose wings you have come for refuge."

13 Then she said, "Let me find favor in your sight, my lord; for you have comforted me, and have spoken kindly to your maidservant, though I am not like one of your maidservants."

14 Now Boaz said to her at mealtime, "Come here, and eat of the bread, and dip your piece of bread in the vinegar." So she sat beside the reapers, and he passed parched *grain* to her; and she ate and was satisfied, and kept some back. 15 And when she rose up to glean, Boaz commanded his young men, saying, "Let her glean even among the sheaves, and do not reproach her. 16 Also let *grain* from the bundles fall purposely for her; leave *it* that she may glean, and do not rebuke her."

17 So she gleaned in the field until evening, and beat out what she had gleaned, and it was about an ephah of barley. 18 Then she took *it* up and went into the city, and her mother-in-law saw what she had gleaned.

So she brought out and gave to her what she had kept back after she had been satisfied.

19 And her mother-in-law said to her, "Where have you gleaned today? And where did you work? Blessed be the one who took notice of you."

So she told her mother-in-law with whom she had worked, and said, "The man's name with whom I worked today *is* Boaz."

20 Then Naomi said to her daughter-in-law, "Blessed *be* he of the LORD, who has not forsaken His kindness to the living and the dead!" And Naomi said to her, "This man *is* a relation of ours, one of our close relatives."

21 Ruth the Moabitess said, "He also said to me, 'You shall stay close by my young men until they have finished all my harvest.'"

22 And Naomi said to Ruth her daughter-in-law, "It *is* good, my daughter, that you go out with his young women, and that people do not meet you in any other field." 23 So she stayed close by the young women of Boaz, to glean until the end of barley harvest and wheat harvest; and she dwelt with her mother-in-law.

Grace

chapter three

A Simple Promise

Sledge — a heavy plank of wood with small stones or sharp metal inserted in the bottom used to help break straw away from grain by dragging it around the threshing floor.

God had blessed the field of Boaz with an abundance of barley. Once his barley had been harvested it was transported in carts to the threshing floor not far from the field. A threshing floor in this biblical time was a large area of earth or stone that had been pounded down to make a large smooth floor. The stalks of barley were spread out over the floor where an animal would be led over it to trample out the grains.[a]

Although a threshing floor is made for harvest, it is mentioned several places in the Bible for some different purposes. The caravan of Joseph, his family, and the Egyptians stopped to camp at a threshing floor to mourn for Jacob before burying him. King David was also told by the Lord to purchase the threshing floor of Ornan the Jebusite, and build an altar there for burnt offerings and peace offerings so that a plague would be lifted from the people of the kingdom.[b] When God answered his prayers, David made that place, which was on Mount Moriah, the location of the Temple.[c]

In these instances, the threshing floor had become a place of mourning, a place of offering for sin, and eventually a place of prayer and worship. And in this story, the threshing floor would become a place where Boaz would soon have a very special encounter in fulfilling God's plan.

The relationship between Naomi and Ruth had become more than closeness through tragedy. Naomi was not just grateful for Ruth's care and devotion; she loved her as dearly as one of her own sons. Ruth could have left, pursued her own interests, or secured her own future. Certainly there were young men who would be interested in her back in Moab or even in Bethlehem, but Ruth had made a vow to Naomi never to leave her, never to be separated from her except by death. Knowing this, Naomi's priority now was for Ruth to be secure with a family of her own. By following Naomi's instructions Ruth had been safe in Boaz' field, but the barley and wheat harvests would soon be over.

Threshing Floor

a   Holman Bible Dictionary — "Agriculture."
b   I Chronicles 21:18–22.
c   I Chronicles 22:1.

Right now it was the time to "winnow" the barley. This would be done by throwing the barley up in the air from a shovel or fan so that it would be separated from the broken straw and lightweight debris, which was carried off by the wind.[d] The best time to do this was in the evening or during the night when the west wind was blowing from the Mediterranean Sea. The west wind was preferred over the stronger north wind and the gusty east wind.[e]

The workers would have their evening meal there at the threshing floor, and when the work was done Boaz and his chosen men would guard the winnowed barley. Threshing floors filled with grain were very inviting to thieves,[f] so Boaz, the grandson of a military leader, would sleep there that night with his men. The harvest had great value and it was vital that it be kept secure.

Since Naomi was a relative of Boaz she knew what he would be doing at the evening of the winnowing. This was the perfect time and place for Ruth to have a private conversation with Boaz, away from the other maidens and workers.

Naomi looked into Ruth's trusting eyes. "My daughter, shall I not seek security for you, that it may be well with you? Now Boaz, whose young women you were with, is he not our relative? In fact, he is winnowing barley tonight at the threshing floor."[g] Naomi's courage is surfacing in her unselfish motive to see Ruth secure in a marriage, which offered the greatest protection and an opportunity to have children. Naomi doesn't seem to feel abandoned anymore, and rather than being focused on all that she had lost, she actively plans for Ruth's future happiness.

d   Easton's Bible Dictionary, "Agriculture — Fan."
e   Easton's Bible Dictionary — "Winnow."
f   1 Samuel 23:1.

g   Ruth 3:1–2.

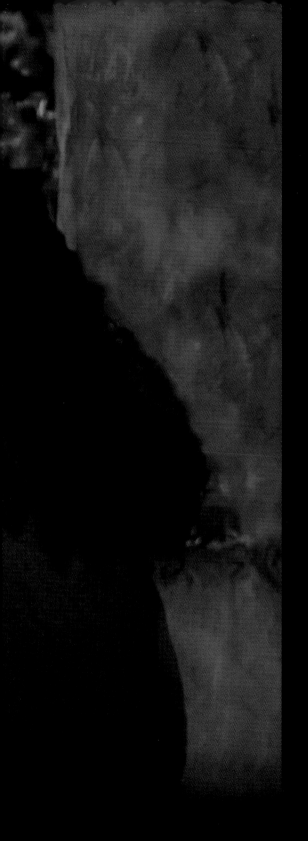

In her devotion, Ruth would do anything Naomi asked her to do. As if preparing Ruth for a wedding, Naomi guided her to wash and anoint herself with perfume and to put on her best clothing. Naomi gave her specific instructions of what she should do every step of the way before and after approaching Boaz. These instructions included how to petition Boaz to redeem her. The importance of carrying on Elimelech's name and his family's duty of marriage to a widow without children were two important laws of the time and stood at the heart of Ruth's petition. Yet this proper act of petition was a risky one for Ruth. She would be placing both her life and personal honor in Boaz' hands.

Sheltered Under His Wing
It was evening as Ruth stood on the top of the hill, the Mediterranean wind blowing through her perfumed hair. The moon and stars were shining bright over the little town of Bethlehem. She looked down at the busy workers throwing barley to the air in the dancing firelight.

Soon they finished and began to rejoice in a meal of celebration. Ruth descended the slope staying in the darkness of the night and approached the threshing floor. She came just close enough to watch Boaz but far enough away for no one to sense her presence. Silently she rejoiced with them. God had been so favorable to her, a maidservant, and had blessed Naomi and her greatly through the valiant man Boaz.

The hearty meal and all the rejoicing would have brought a contented tiredness to Boaz. Ruth watched him go to the end of the pile of grain where he had prepared a place for himself to rest and waited for him to fall asleep.

It was near midnight and the only sounds were the crackling of the fire and the leaves whispering in the night breeze. Following Naomi's instructions, Ruth got up and went quietly to where Boaz lay. She had a very important question to ask Boaz and may have been a little afraid, but she took the next step of Naomi's instructions. Ruth lifted the covering over Boaz' feet and knelt down and softly laid

herself there as a gesture of humility. Also by placing a portion of his covering over her, Ruth was symbolically asking for his protection by marriage.

As she lay there she may have thought back to what a wonderful day it was when Boaz first noticed her and made her like one of his handmaidens. It was a day that Ruth would always hold dear to her heart. Unlike the dating traditions of today, Ruth and Boaz would have only seen or spoken to one another before this night in the company of others as they worked in the field.

Her perfume enveloped Boaz as he slept. Suddenly he became startled and he turned to find a woman at his feet. Alert for possible thieves or danger, he immediately sat up and asked her who she was. Immediately Ruth responded,

"…I am Ruth, your maidservant. Take your maidservant under your wing, for you are a close relative…"

–Ruth 3:9

As Boaz had noted when he spoke with her that first day in the field, Ruth had already proclaimed her conversion to God "under whose wings" she had sought refuge. Now she wanted to come under the wing of the man Boaz. By saying this, as the widow of Mahlon, she was asking him to redeem the land of Elimelech's family by marrying her.

Boaz was astonished at her goodness and selflessness. Not only had she given up her own family and native land to follow Naomi, she was willing to give herself in marriage to him for redemption of Elimelech's land. What faith this young woman had! She didn't follow after younger men or riches but humbled herself before a man of an older generation in trying to follow the Jewish laws of redemption. Boaz blessed her for this.

There had been a closer relative of Elimelech's family all along who had the first right to purchase his estate and in doing so, to marry Ruth. And because Boaz was a righteous man he followed the laws of God. Boaz told Ruth not to be afraid, if the relative that had the first right would not redeem her by the law then as the Lord lives he would redeem her himself!

Boaz said she should rest there that night, again showing concern for her safety, and in the morning he would handle the matter. It was in Boaz' hands now and Ruth laid back down at his feet secure in his promise. That night on the threshing floor in the field of the tiny town of Bethlehem an honorable commitment was made between Boaz and Ruth with God as their witness. A star seemed to shine brighter and the sweet, innocent bleating of a lamb came from a shepherd's flock nearby.

In the very early morning before the sun would light up the sky, Ruth got up and prepared to leave. Lest someone speak poorly of her, Boaz cautioned her not to let anyone see that a woman had come to the threshing floor, but before she left, Boaz wanted her to take something to Naomi. He told her to hold out her shawl and he poured barley grains into it one measure at a time.

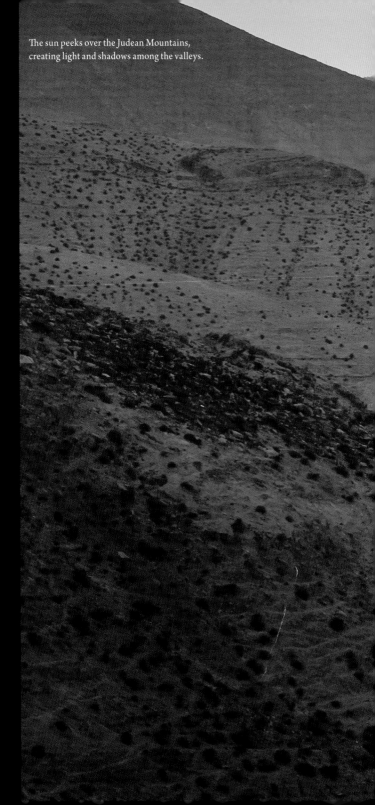

The sun peeks over the Judean Mountains, creating light and shadows among the valleys.

A reconstructed watchtower no longer used. A watchtower provided a high, safe place from which a guard could observe the surrounding area.

One measure . . . two . . . three . . . four . . . five . . . there seemed to be
a purpose in the amount of measures. It echoed an earlier biblical
event from the time of Joseph. In the day that the children of Israel
were allowed to farm Pharaoh's land in Egypt, Joseph had measured
out grain seed for each tribe. He proclaimed, "Indeed I have bought
you and your land this day for Pharaoh. Look, here is seed for you,
and you shall sow the land. And it shall come to pass in the harvest
that you shall give one-fifth to Pharaoh. Four-fifths shall be your own,
as seed for the field and for your food, for those of your households
and as food for your little ones."[h]

By God's direction Joseph had saved grain over a period of seven
years to provide for the seven-year famine to come. Boaz, under
God's direction, was similarly providing for the family of Elimelech.
He poured a sixth and final measure into Ruth's shawl and sent her
on her way.

h   Genesis 47:23–24.

A GIFT OF SIX

Ruth hurried to the city and reached home before the break of dawn. Naomi, not able to see her clearly asked, "Is that you, my daughter?"[i] Ruth presented herself to Naomi with the news of all that had happened with Boaz that night. God's plan had been carried out successfully by these two dear widows for His purpose.

With excitement, Ruth poured out the six measures of barley from her shawl and she told Naomi that Boaz did not want her to go empty-handed to her mother-in law. Naomi's face glowed from the message.

Some say the six measures represented the six members of Elimelech's family. Whatever the meaning, Naomi received it as a token of a promise from Boaz, just as Rahab received the token promise of salvation for her and her family from Joshua and Caleb by the scarlet cord. Naomi knew this token from Boaz meant that he would perform the duty of redemption according to the law. Boaz would settle what had been left undone by the nearer kinsman.

Ruth looked at her mother for the next step. With an assuring smile Naomi instructed her, "Sit still, my daughter, until you know how the matter will turn out; for the man will not rest until he has concluded the matter this day."[j]

i   Ruth 3:16
j   Ruth 3:18

Ruth

3

Ruth's Redemption Assured

[1] Then Naomi her mother-in-law said to her, "My daughter, shall I not seek security for you, that it may be well with you? [2] Now Boaz, whose young women you were with, *is he* not our relative? In fact, he is winnowing barley tonight at the threshing floor. [3] Therefore wash yourself and anoint yourself, put on your *best* garment and go down to the threshing floor; *but do* not make yourself known to the man until he has finished eating and drinking. [4] Then it shall be, when he lies down, that you shall notice the place where he lies; and you shall go in, uncover his feet, and lie down; and he will tell you what you should do."

5 And she said to her, "All that you say to me I will do."

6 So she went down to the threshing floor and did according to all that her mother-in-law instructed her. 7 And after Boaz had eaten and drunk, and his heart was cheerful, he went to lie down at the end of the heap of grain; and she came softly, uncovered his feet, and lay down.

8 Now it happened at midnight that the man was startled, and turned himself; and there, a woman was lying at his feet. 9 And he said, "Who *are* you?"

So she answered, "I *am* Ruth, your maidservant. Take your maidservant under your wing,[a] for you are a close relative."

10 Then he said, "Blessed *are* you of the LORD, my daughter! For you have shown more kindness at the end than at the beginning, in that you did not go after young men, whether poor or rich. 11 And now, my daughter, do not fear. I will do for you all that you request, for all the people of my town know that you *are* a virtuous woman. 12 Now it is true that I *am* a close relative; however, there is a relative closer than I. 13 Stay this night, and in the morning it shall be *that* if he will perform the duty of a close relative for you—good; let him do it. But if he does not want to perform the duty for you, then I will perform the duty for you, *as* the LORD lives! Lie down until morning."

14 So she lay at his feet until morning, and she arose before one could recognize another. Then he said, "Do not let it be known that the woman came to the threshing floor." 15 Also he said, "Bring the shawl that *is* on you and hold it." And when she held it, he measured six *ephahs* of barley, and laid *it* on her. Then she[b] went into the city.

16 When she came to her mother-in-law, she said, "*Is* that you, my daughter?"

Then she told her all that the man had done for her. 17 And she said, "These six *ephahs* of barley he gave me; for he said to me, 'Do not go empty-handed to your mother-in-law.'"

18 Then she said, "Sit still, my daughter, until you know how the matter will turn out; for the man will not rest until he has concluded the matter this day."

a   Ruth 3:9 Or *Spread the corner of your garment over your maidservant*

b   Ruth 3:15 Many Hebrew manuscripts, Syriac, and Vulgate read *she*; Masoretic Text, Septuagint, and Targum read *he*.

It was not long after Ruth had reached home that Boaz went up to the city gate. This is the place where decisions were made and proclaimed throughout the city. It served as a court of law. On the gates of some cities the law that God gave through Moses was written on and above the gate.[a]

Boaz was there to comply with the law for the redemption of Elimelech's land and family. While at the gate, the closer relative of Elimelech passed by. Boaz greeted him and asked him to sit down there at the gate. This meant that he wanted to have a proper meeting of business with the relative. To make it official, Boaz asked ten of the elders of the city to come and sit down as well. They would be the witnesses of the matter.

a   Smith's Bible Dictionary — "Gate" and Deuteronomy 6:9.

It is important to note that Abraham's nephew Lot, the patriarch of Ruth, was also one who "sat in the gate." It was the gate of the city of Sodom, and the people there did not want any business with righteousness, but because of the prayer of Abraham, who was called a friend of God three times in the Bible, Lot was spared from the perilous judgment to come. And now at Bethlehem's gate, the uncertain future of Ruth and Naomi depended on what would happen next between Boaz and the close relative.

The stillness of the waiting was the greatest challenge of all for these two widows. Would Boaz be able to take the place of the close relative? Would they be redeemed at all? God had shown favor to Ruth and Naomi. Would He then secure their future through Boaz and give them an inheritance?

her tragic losses and Ruth was well-known in the gate for her virtue. She had only worked in Boaz' field just as Naomi told her, and every day she would walk home through the city gate, not once giving any interest to any romantic looks young men would give her as she passed by.

The close relative gave his answer, "I will redeem it."[d] There may have been some disappointment in the crowd from his answer. Some of them knew that meant Ruth could not belong to Boaz.

But Boaz had his presentation well thought out in a way that there would be no question of who would be the redeemer. He then said to the close relative, "On the day you buy the field from the hand of Naomi, you must also buy it from Ruth the Moabitess, the wife of the dead, to perpetuate the name of the dead through his inheritance."[e]

This changed everything. If he only had to buy the land from Naomi it may have been different, but he would have to buy it from Ruth as well. The close relative was not in a position to take a wife because he was already married. And he couldn't "perpetuate the name" of Elimelech by bearing children through Ruth. She was a Moabitess and it would compromise the inheritance of his own children.

The close relative answered Boaz, "I cannot redeem it for myself, lest I ruin my own inheritance. You redeem my right of redemption for yourself, for I cannot redeem it."[f]

d   Ibid..

e   Ruth 4:5.
f   Ruth 4:6.

By following the law, Boaz had cleared the way so that he could rightfully become the redeemer and buy back the land. He had made it clear that buying back the land meant continuing the inheritance of Elimelech through Ruth.

To confirm this in all the eyes of those watching, the close relative took off his sandal and gave it to Boaz. This old custom was considered a confirmation to the children of Israel of giving his right to Boaz for the purchase and redemption. The close relative was the rightful redeemer but could not be jeopardized and so he was replaced by Boaz who was willing to make Naomi and Ruth co-heirs of his own estate.

Then Boaz addressed the elders and the people proclaiming, "You are witnesses this day that I have bought all that was Elimelech's, and all that was Chilion's and Mahlon's, from the hand of Naomi. Moreover, Ruth the Moabitess, the widow of Mahlon, I have acquired as my wife, to perpetuate the name of the dead through his inheritance, that the name of the dead may not be cut off from among his brethren and from his position at the gate. You are witnesses this day."[g]

Because of Boaz' faithfulness, Elimelech's name, usually translated "My God is King," and his position at the gate would not be cut off. The purchase was a victory. The elders and the people began rejoicing. They had been watching God work in the lives of Naomi, Boaz, and Ruth, and their victory was a victory for them all.

g   Ruth 4:9–10.

The people rejoiced at the thought that God would bring an heir through Boaz and they blessed him saying, "We are witnesses. The Lord make the woman who is coming to your house like Rachel and Leah, the two who built the house of Israel; and may you prosper in Ephrathah and be famous in Bethlehem. May your house be like the house of Perez, whom Tamar bore to Judah, because of the offspring which the Lord will give you from this young woman."[h]

h   Ruth 4:11–12.

Lift up your heads, O you gates!

A Blessed Future

Ruth had waited patiently for Boaz to come back, and he did. He came back as her bridegroom. Truly this was a match made in heaven. God's commitment to bring them together and keep them together was by His own hand . . . for His plan that all nations should be blessed through the seed of Abraham was still in effect.

The beauty of this union was kissed by God's love, and the marriage of Boaz and Ruth has never been forgotten to this day. After Boaz took Ruth to be his wife, God continued His plan and blessed them with a son.

This was also a blessed day for Naomi, for this son, born of the same blood as her husband's, would live to carry on for the sons she had lost. God had not forgotten her place as a mother in the living story of His redemption.

The rejoicing was for Naomi this time and the women blessed the Lord for what He had done, saying, "Blessed be the Lord, who has not left you this day without a close relative; and may his name be famous in Israel! And may he be to you a restorer of life and a nourisher of your old age; for your daughter-in-law, who loves you, who is better to you than seven sons, has borne him."[i]

God had taken the torn pieces of Naomi's life and molded them into a new life handed to her by Boaz, her redeemer, and Ruth, a loving and faithful daughter who was worth more than seven sons. And this blessing, this son, was named Obed, "the servant," because he would serve to fill Naomi's renewed embrace of hope.

The hills of Judea between Jerusalem and Jericho come to life after a heavy rain; the desert and mountains are spotted with vegetation, flowers, and remarkable color of the yellow Faktorowsky's Aaronsonia.

The lineage of this particular family is woven into the genealogy of the promised Messiah, Yeshua, Jesus the Christ, and is recorded in the New Testament Book of Matthew:

And Boaz begot Obed by Ruth,

Obed begot Jesse,

and Jesse begot David the King.

David begot Solomon. . . .

Solomon begot Rehoboam,

Rehoboam begot Abijah,

and Abijah begot Asa.

Asa begot Jehoshaphat,

and Jehoshaphat begot Joram,

and Joram begot Uzziah.

Uzziah begot Jotham,

Jotham begot Ahaz,

and Ahaz begot Hezekiah.

Hezekiah begot Manasseh,

Manasseh begot Amon,

and Amon begot Josiah.

Josiah begot Jeconiah . . .

Jeconiah begot Shealtiel,

and Shealtiel begot Zerubbabel.

Zerubbabel begot Abiud,

Abiud begot Eliakim,

and Eliakim begot Azor.

Azor begot Zadok,

Zadok begot Achim,

and Achim begot Eliud.

Eliud begot Eleazar,

Eleazar begot Matthan,

and Matthan begot Jacob.

And Jacob begot Joseph the husband of Mary, of whom was born Jesus who is called Christ.[j]

_____

j .   Matthew 1:5-16.

Boaz Redeems Ruth

[1] Now Boaz went up to the gate and sat down there; and behold, the close relative of whom Boaz had spoken came by. So Boaz said, "Come aside, friend,[a] sit down here." So he came aside and sat down. [2] And he took ten men of the elders of the city, and said, "Sit down here." So they sat down. [3] Then he said to the close relative, "Naomi, who has come back from the country of Moab, sold the piece of land which *belonged* to our brother Elimelech. [4] And I thought to inform you, saying, 'Buy *it* back in the presence of the inhabitants and the elders of my people. If you will redeem *it*, redeem *it*; but if you[b] will not redeem *it*, *then* tell me, that I may know; for *there is* no one but you to redeem *it*, and I *am* next after you.'"

a   Ruth 4:1 Hebrew *peloni almoni*; literally *so and so*
b   Ruth 4:4 Following many Hebrew manuscripts, Septuagint, Syriac, Targum, and Vulgate; Masoretic Text reads *he.*

And he said, "I will redeem *it*."

5 Then Boaz said, "On the day you buy the field from the hand of Naomi, you must also buy *it* from Ruth the Moabitess, the wife of the dead, to perpetuate[c] the name of the dead through his inheritance."

6 And the close relative said, "I cannot redeem *it* for myself, lest I ruin my own inheritance. You redeem my right of redemption for yourself, for I cannot redeem *it*."

7 Now this *was the custom* in former times in Israel concerning redeeming and exchanging, to confirm anything: one man took off his sandal and gave *it* to the other, and this *was* a confirmation in Israel.

8 Therefore the close relative said to Boaz, "Buy *it* for yourself." So he took off his sandal. 9 And Boaz said to the elders and all the people, "You *are* witnesses this day that I have bought all that was Elimelech's, and all that *was* Chilion's and Mahlon's, from the hand of Naomi. 10 Moreover, Ruth the Moabitess, the widow of Mahlon, I have acquired as my wife, to perpetuate the name of the dead through his inheritance, that the name of the dead may not be cut off from among his brethren and from his position at the gate.[d] You *are* witnesses this day."

11 And all the people who *were* at the gate, and the elders, said, "*We* are witnesses. The LORD make the woman who is coming to your house like Rachel and Leah, the two who built the house of Israel; and may you prosper in Ephrathah and be famous in Bethlehem. 12 May your house be like the house of Perez, whom Tamar bore to Judah, because of the offspring which the LORD will give you from this young woman."

Descendants of Boaz and Ruth

13 So Boaz took Ruth and she became his wife; and when he went in to her, the LORD gave her conception, and she bore a son. 14 Then the women said to Naomi, "Blessed *be* the LORD, who has not left you this day without a close relative; and may his name be famous in Israel! 15 And may he be to you a restorer of life and a nourisher of your old age; for your daughter-in-law, who loves you, who is better to you than seven sons, has borne him." 16 Then Naomi took the child and laid him on her bosom, and became a nurse to him. 17 Also the neighbor women gave him a name, saying, "There is a son born to Naomi." And they called his name Obed. He *is* the father of Jesse, the father of David.

18 Now this *is* the genealogy of Perez: Perez begot Hezron; 19 Hezron begot Ram, and Ram begot Amminadab; 20 Amminadab begot Nahshon, and Nahshon begot Salmon;[e] 21 Salmon begot Boaz, and Boaz begot Obed; 22 Obed begot Jesse, and Jesse begot David.

---

c   Ruth 4:5 Literally *raise up*

d   Ruth 4:10 Probably his civic office

e   Ruth 4:20 Hebrew *Salmah*

God's love story through the lives of Naomi, Ruth, and Boaz helps us understand that during the famines of heart and soul He can fill our needs and our desires from the most unlikely circumstances.

As widows, both Naomi and Ruth had lost their former identities through loss and crisis, but by God's direction He birthed a meaningful relationship for each of them in their identity with Him. He had surrounded them in their abandonment with the sense of His presence and showed them that nothing is impossible.

The journey that led them by and to God revealed their relationship to be more than a confirmation that He is God . . . it was an acceptance of Him . . . for Naomi an acceptance that He loved her all along . . . for Ruth an acceptance that the God of her new beloved mother loved her, a foreigner, just the same.

God used the kinsman redeemer Boaz to demonstrate how He gives to those who seek what has been left for them and fills their arms with His bountiful harvest, a provision of love through salvation in His Son Jesus Christ.

From here we see God's beautiful story continue through the blended family lineage that brings us the gift of His only begotten Son, who remains forever matchless!

> Therefore God also has highly exalted Him, and given Him a name which is above every name, that at the name of Jesus every knee should bow, of those in heaven, and of those on earth, and of those under the earth, and that every tongue should confess that Jesus Christ is Lord, to the glory of God the Father.
>
> —Philippians 2:9–11

ABOUT KENNETH BERG
Ken has traveled extensively throughout the Holy Land and the Middle East for over three decades producing award-winning television programs based on the bible. His studies and degree in fine art serves as a background to his creative eye.

Ken was raised as a minister's son in New York City. After serving in the motion picture division of the US Army, he moved to California, where he worked in Hollywood for a Christian advertising agency. He has gleaned his experience as a producer, director, graphic artist, and photographer in places such as New York, Hollywood, California, Europe, and throughout the Middle East.

His passion for telling biblical stories within authentic locations is reinforced all the more by his commitment to serving the Lord through his business, Berg Productions, Inc. Berg Productions produces such programs as "Zola Levitt Presents" and "The Nazareth Jesus Knew," which can be seen on one or more of the national Christian networks. His full-service production company has also produced all of the video incorporated in "Passages," a national interactive exhibit that presents a history of the Bible.

Ken's photos have been featured in *US Camera and Travel* magazine, and he has garnered over 30 awards for his work in television and film.

It is with this extensive background and experience that he was able to put together this unique photo book with stellar high-definition photos giving the viewer a realistic look into the past through the story of Ruth. There are many beautiful stories in the Bible that Ken hopes to make into works of art from his treasure of photographs rich in authenticity and vision.

About Brenda Carol Duff

Little did her mother know that the first and middle names she chose for her would actually describe two of Brenda's favorite interests. Brenda from the comic strip "Brenda Star," a redheaded reporter who loved to research a story, and Carol because her mom wanted her to sing. She's been singing since the age of four.

Research has been a part of Brenda's life for many years. She had the privilege of working for Liberty University for the dean of students and the president of the college, and also for radio syndication. During this time she took a few courses and majored in psychology.

She also worked in the City Secretary's Office of Irving, Texas and often researched ordinances and resolutions. Later she would work for an underwriter of commercial land loans, where she did a great deal of research on the land and principles of loan requests.

Brenda was able to immerse herself further into the Christian media world during the late 90s to 2002 as the office manager and human resource specialist in the fast-moving environment of Daystar Television.

When she came on board at Berg Productions, Ken Berg gave her the opportunity to learn about film production by allowing her to assist on shoots. He also gave her a chance to express her enthusiasm about certain topics by affording her the opportunity to write copy for his website and other projects. It turns out that research and writing are a good combination for her. She will always appreciate his encouragement.

Ken's photo book, *I Am Ruth — A Story of Loss, Love, and Redemption*, was particularly impressive to her because of her experience in working with several women's groups. She soon learned the different challenges women face today, as well as share in the many joys that God brought their way. However, this is not just a book for women. We receive positive feedback from men and children as well.

The Bible is without a doubt the most interesting subject to research and put words to paper. When it is from His Word and through His Spirit, the motivation is never ending.

BERG PRODUCTIONS has produced biblically based television

programs and films, shot primarily in the Holy Land for over three decades. Our purpose is to present the Living Word within the culture and context of Bible times, using the best of today's technology.

Projects produced in the Holy Land have included:

"Zola Levitt Presents," a weekly telecast broadcast internationally

"The Nazareth Jesus Knew," a weekly telecast hosted by Pat Boone

"Miracles," a one-hour music special featuring Dino Kartsonakis

"His Last Days," a one-hour dramatic film featuring Dallas Holm

"Jehovah's Treasure," a television special featuring David Dolan and narrated by Max McLean

"Upon This Rock," a TV special narrated by Efrem Zimbalist Jr.

Projects produced domestically have included:

"To Life," a weekly health program for the Cooper Fitness Center hosted by Dr. Kenneth Cooper

"The Witness," a weekly telecast for Christ for the Nations hosted by Dennis Lindsay

Video segments for "Passages," a Bible exhibit that has toured the United States and abroad

For information about Berg Productions visit bergproductions.com

f Facebook at facebook.com/KennethBergCollection,

t Twitter at twitter.com/ImKennethBerg

New Leaf Press

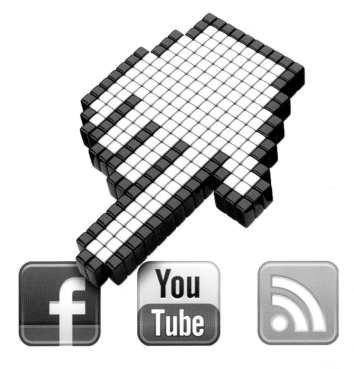

Connect with New Leaf Press®

newleafpress.net

An Imprint of New Leaf Publishing Group

facebook.com/**masterbooks**
twitter.com/**masterbooks4u**
youtube.com/**nlpgvideo**

nlpgblogs.com
nlpgvideos.com

join us at **Creation**Conversations.com

Connecting Christians who believe in Biblical Creation